HILARIOUS JOKES
FOR

YEAR OLD KIDS

A Message From the Publisher

Hello! My name is Hayden and I am the owner of Hayden Fox Publishing, the publishing house that brought you this title.

My hope is that you and your young comedian love this book and enjoy every single page. If you do, please think about **giving us your honest feedback via a review on Amazon**. It may only take a moment, but it really does mean the world for small businesses like mine.

Even if you happen to not like this title, please let us know the reason in your review so that we may improve this title for the future and serve you better.

The mission of Hayden Fox is to create premium content for children that will help them increase their confidence and grow their imaginations while having tons of fun along the way.

Without you, however, this would not be possible, so we sincerely thank you for your purchase and for supporting our company mission.

Sincerely,
Hayden Fox

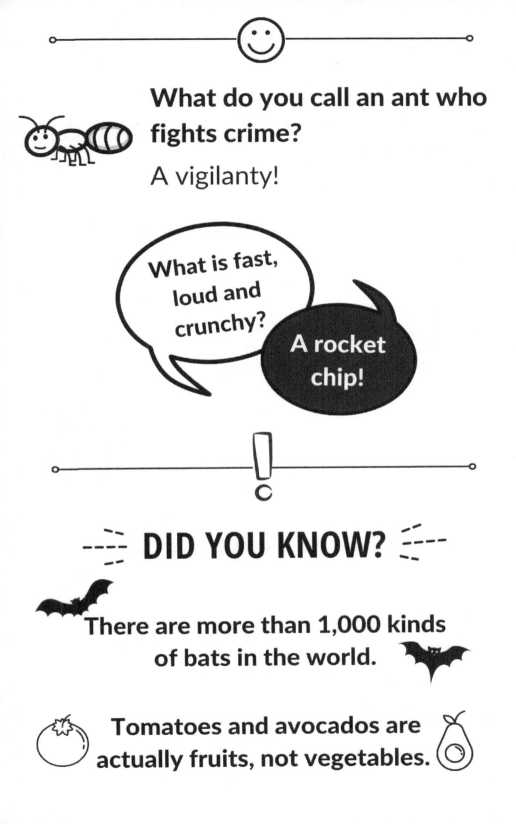

What do you call an ant who fights crime?

A vigilanty!

What is fast, loud and crunchy?

A rocket chip!

DID YOU KNOW?

There are more than 1,000 kinds of bats in the world.

Tomatoes and avocados are actually fruits, not vegetables.

RIDDLES

I have two hands but am unable to clap. What am I?
A clock

What falls while never getting hurt?
Snow

Seth at Sainsbury's sells thick socks

TONGUE TWISTER

Knock Knock!

Who's there?
Atch.
Atch who?
Bless you!

What is a man with a shovel called?

Doug.

How do bees get to school?

They take the school buzz.

DID YOU KNOW?

Caterpillars have 12 eyes!

Horses and cows sleep standing up.

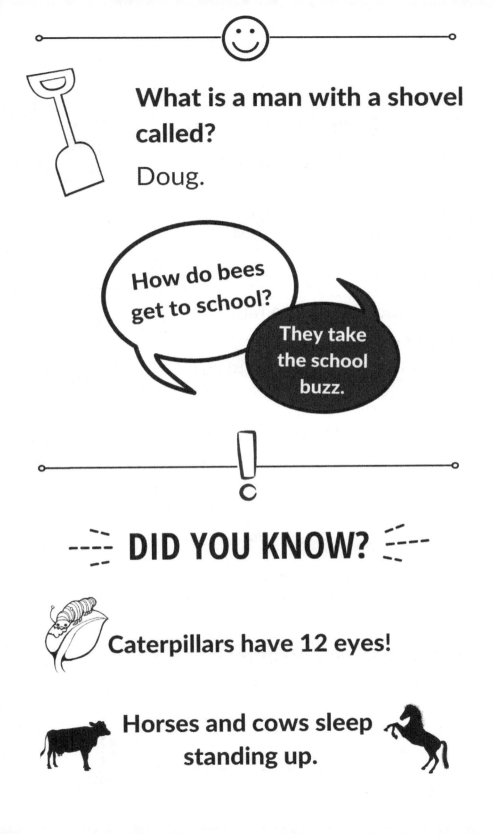

Clean clams crammed in clean cans.

What looks just like half a loaf of bread?

The other half of a loaf of bread.

What has no leg but has a foot?

A ruler.

⫶⫶ DID YOU KNOW? ⫶⫶

If there was a straight road to space, it would only take 1 hour to drive there.

Slugs have four noses.

What do you call a rabbit that tells good jokes?

A funny bunny.

How does a train like to eat?

By going chewwww chewww!

Who's there?

Ears.

Ears who?

Ears some more knock knock jokes for you!

Knock Knock!

RIDDLES

I have a long trunk, but I am not an elephant. What am I?
A tree

I have legs but cannot walk. What am I?
A table

What did the dog say to the sandpaper?

"Ruff!"

Knock Knock!

Who's there?
Knock.
Knock who?
Knock, Knock!

Knock Knock!

Who's there?
Tail.
Tail who?
Tail all your friends this joke.

TONGUE TWISTER

Santa's Short Suit Shrunk

RIDDLES

How can you keep a skunk from smelling?
Hold its nose.

Where do cows travel on business trips?
Moo York.

What kind of witches like the beach?
Sand-witches

The difference between a piano and a fish?

You can tune a piano but you can't tuna fish!

DID YOU KNOW?

Dogs' hearing is 10 times better than a human's.

Apples float on water.

What do you call a fairy that has just fallen in the garbage?

Stinker bell.

RIDDLES

What's the reason why your nose is not twelve inches long?

Because then it would be a foot.

Does this shop sport short socks with spots?

TONGUE TWISTER

Knock Knock!

Who's there?

Art.

Art Who?

R2-D2.

What type of sickness does a book have?

Book worms!

What is a rock's favorite kind of music?

Rock and roll

☰ DID YOU KNOW? ☰

4 Number four is the only one with the same amount of letters.

 Your heart is about the same size as your fist.

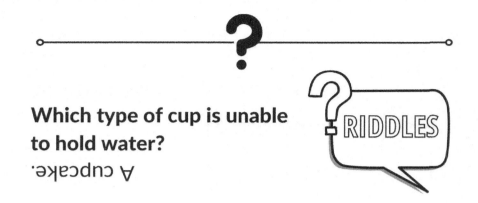

Which type of cup is unable to hold water?
A cupcake.

I have two heads, six legs, four eyes, and a tail. What am I?
A cowboy riding his horse.

Knock Knock!

Who's there?
Lego.
Lego who?
Lego to the movies!

I scream, you scream, we all scream for ice cream!

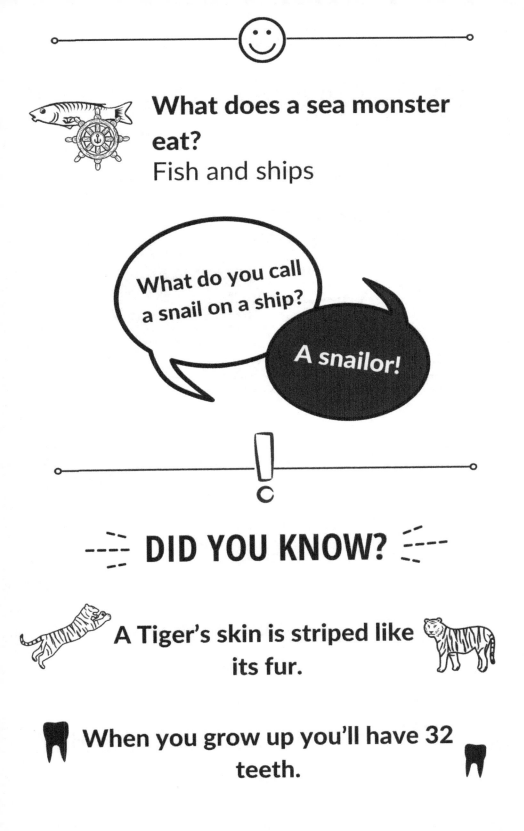

What does a sea monster eat?
Fish and ships

What do you call a snail on a ship?

A snailor!

DID YOU KNOW?

A Tiger's skin is striped like its fur.

When you grow up you'll have 32 teeth.

Why is a bad joke like a pencil?

Because it has no point.

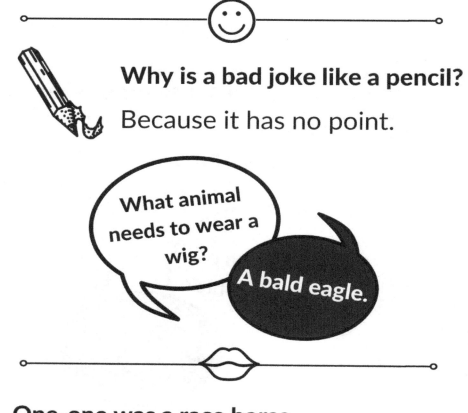

What animal needs to wear a wig?

A bald eagle.

One-one was a race horse.
Two-two was one too.
One-one won one race.
Two-two won one too.

TONGUE TWISTER

Who's there?

Hank.

Hank who?

Hank you for letting me in!

Knock Knock!

Willy's real rear wheel

Knock Knock!

Who's there?
Let us.
Let us who?
Let us in and you will find out!

The world's longest French fry is 34-inches long.

Which two keys are not allowed to open doors?
Don-keys and mon-keys.

I have three letters. I read the same forward and backward. I know you'll get this answer; I know you'll see. It's a word that's important to you and me. What word am I?
Eye.

Why is Peter Pan always flying?

Because he NEVER lands!

What has two legs but can't walk?

A pair of pants.

What kind of bird is always sad?

Blue jays.

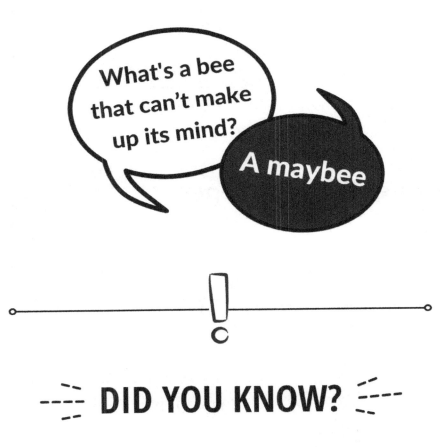

What's a bee that can't make up its mind?

A maybee

 DID YOU KNOW?

A cat named Félicette has gone into space.

Which letter of the English alphabet is also considered an insect?

The letter "b" (bee).

Which letter of the alphabet contains the most water?

"C"

Pirates Private Property

Who's there?
Scold.
Scold who?
Scold out here so let me in!

What did the tiger say to her cub on his birthday?

It's ROAR birthday.

Where do sheep go to get haircuts?

The baa-baa shop.

--‑ DID YOU KNOW? ‑--

 Turtles can breathe through their butts.

It might not look like it, but penguins have knees!

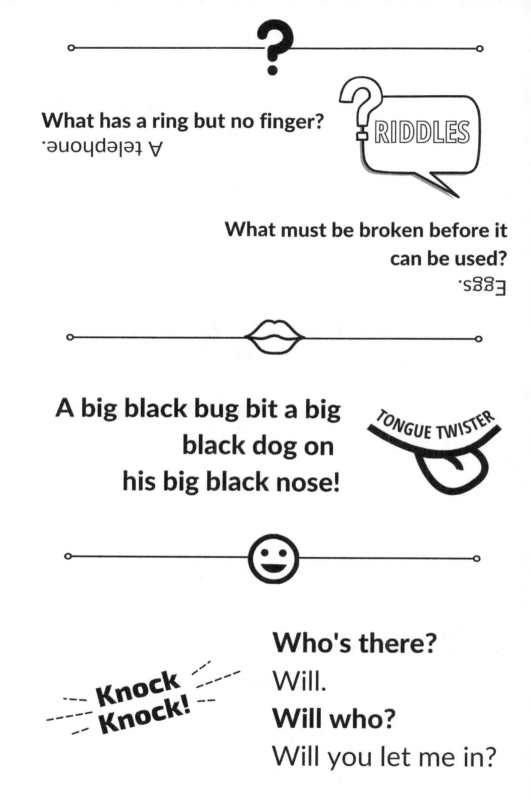

What has a ring but no finger?
A telephone.

RIDDLES

What must be broken before it can be used?
Eggs.

A big black bug bit a big black dog on his big black nose!

TONGUE TWISTER

Knock Knock!

Who's there?
Will.
Will who?
Will you let me in?

DID YOU KNOW?

Talking to your plants and playing music can help them grow faster.

The average person spends 26 years of their life sleeping! zzZ

She sells sea shells on the sea shore.

TONGUE TWISTER

Knock Knock!

Who's there?
Cat.
Cat who?
Cat you just open this door!

What did the one glue stick say to the other?

Let's stick together.

DID YOU KNOW?

Cotton candy was invented by a dentist.

How much pot, could a pot roast roast, if a pot roast could roast pot.

TONGUE TWISTER

Knock Knock!

Who's there?
Goat.
Goat who?
Goat to the door and see.

What did the finger say to the thumb?

I'm in glove with you!

What dog keeps the best time?

A watch dog.

!

If you eat too many carrots, it is possible for your skin to turn orange.

Betty bought some bitter butter and it made her batter bitter

TONGUE TWISTER

Who's there?
Dishes.
Dishes who?
Dishes me,
who are you?

Knock Knock!

! DID YOU KNOW?

Cockroaches can live for up to 1 week without their heads.

Oranges were originally green.

I wish I were what I was
when I wished
I were what I am.

TONGUE TWISTER

Knock Knock!

Who's there?
Sorry.
Sorry who?
Sorry wrong door!

What do you get when you cross a ball and a cat?

A fur ball.

What did the ghost put on his bagel?

SCREAM cheese!

DID YOU KNOW?

Recycling one glass jar saves enough energy to watch television for 3 hours.

A giraffe has the same number of bones in their neck as humans.

The blue bluebird blinks.

TONGUE TWISTER

Who's there?

Zit.

Zit who?

Zit time to open the door yet?

Knock Knock!

Why did the girl throw a stick of butter?

She wanted to see a butter-fly!

What goes tick-tock and woof-woof?

A watchdog.

My mommy makes me muffins on Mondays.

TONGUE TWISTER

Knock Knock!

Who's there?
Toodle.
Toodle who?
Bye, bye!

What kind of key can never unlock a door?

A monkey

❗ DID YOU KNOW?

Mandarin Chinese is the most popular language in the world.

France is the #1 most-visited country in the world. Spain is #2.

Green glass globes glow greenly.

TONGUE TWISTER

Knock Knock!

Who's there?
Eddie.
Eddie who?
Eddie body home?

What do you get when a cow laughs?

A milkshake.

What is a dog's favorite button on a remote?

Paws

black back bat

TONGUE TWISTER

Knock Knock!

Who's there?
Zany.
Zany who?
Zany body home?

What did the little corn say to the mama corn?

Where is pop corn?

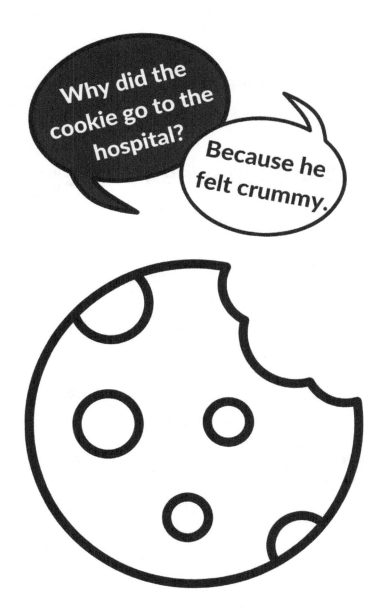

DID YOU KNOW?

You are 1 cm taller when you wake up.

The queen in green screamed.

TONGUE TWISTER

Knock Knock!

Who's there?
Mikey.
Mikey who?
Mikey doesn't fit in the lock!

How do you talk to a giant?

Use big words!

DID YOU KNOW?

Only 10% of people are left-handed.

Snap Crackel Pop,
Snap Crackel Pop,
Snap Crackel Pop

TONGUE TWISTER

Knock Knock!

Who's there?
Bella.
Bella who?
Bella not work so I knock on the door.

How do you make a tissue dance?

You put a little boogie in it.

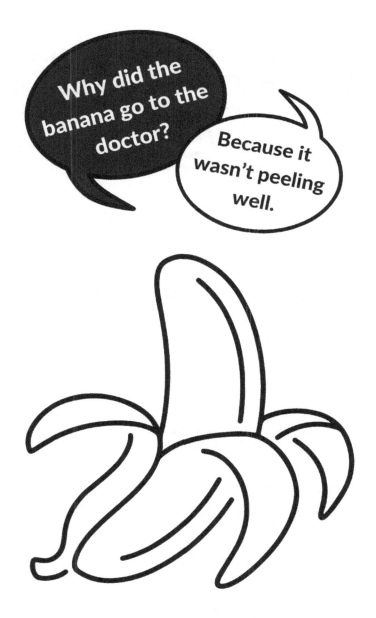

DID YOU KNOW?

Hippopotamus milk is pink.

A piece of standard paper can be folded in half 7 times and that's it!

Knock Knock!

Who's there?
Frank.
Frank who?
Frank you for being my friend!

TONGUE TWISTER

Six slimy snails sailed silently.

! DID YOU KNOW?

No word in the English language rhymes with "month".

All swans in England are owned by the Queen.

Who's there?
Cow
Cow who?
Cows don't say who, they say moooo!

Knock Knock!

Thought I thought of thinking of thanking you.

TONGUE TWISTER

Kid: **What are you doing under there?**

Mom: Under where?

Kid: **Ha ha! You said underwear!!**

What do ghosts like to eat in the summer?

I Scream.

! DID YOU KNOW?

Hippos have such large mouths that a 4ft. child can fit inside of it.

Knock Knock!

Who's there?
Willa.
Willa who?
Willa you marry me?

He threw three balls.

TONGUE TWISTER

Singing Sammy sung songs on sinking sand.

Knock Knock!

Who's there?
Willa.
Willa who?
Willa you marry me?

Knock Knock!

Who's there?
Cheese.
Cheese who?
Cheese a happy girl!

He threw three free throws.

TONGUE TWISTER

Gig whip, gig whip, gig whip, ...

Why did Superman flush the toilet?

Because it was his doody.

What time do ducks wake up?

At the quack of dawn.

Who's there?
Abby.
Abby who?
Abby Valentine's Day!

Who's there?
Happy.
Happy who?
Happy Easter!

Little Mike left his bike at Spike's.

I'll chew and chew until my jaws drop.

Who's there?
Peas.
Peas who?
Peas be my Valentine!

Who's there?
Abbey.
Abbey who?
Abbey birthday to you!

Real rock wall, real rock wall, real rock wall

TONGUE TWISTER

Two tiny tigers take two taxis to town.

What's yellow and looks like pineapple?

A lemon with a new haircut.

What do you call a fly with no wings?

A walk

Who's there?
Gus.
Gus who?
Gus how old I am!

Who's there?
Chris.
Chris who?
Christmas!

Double bubble gum bubbles double.

How do they answer the phone at the paint store?

Yellow!

Why do birds fly south?

It's too far to walk.

Who's there?
Coal.
Coal who?
Coal me if you hear Santa coming.

Who's there?
Elf.
Elf who?
Elf I knock again will you let me in?

How many candy cans can a candy canner can?

Who's there?
Ho, Ho, Ho.
Ho, Ho, Ho who?
Ho, Ho, Ho, Merry Christmas to you!

Who's there?
Holly.
Holly who?
Holly – days are here again!

Wunwun won one race and Tutu won one too.

Where should a dog never go shopping?

A flea market

Who's there?
Voodoo.
Voodoo who?
Voodoo you think
you are?

Who's there?
Donut.
Donut who?
Donut ask me, I just
got here.

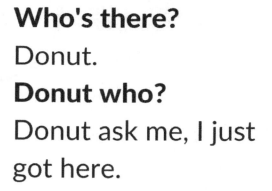

**The big black bug bit
the big black bear.**

TONGUE TWISTER

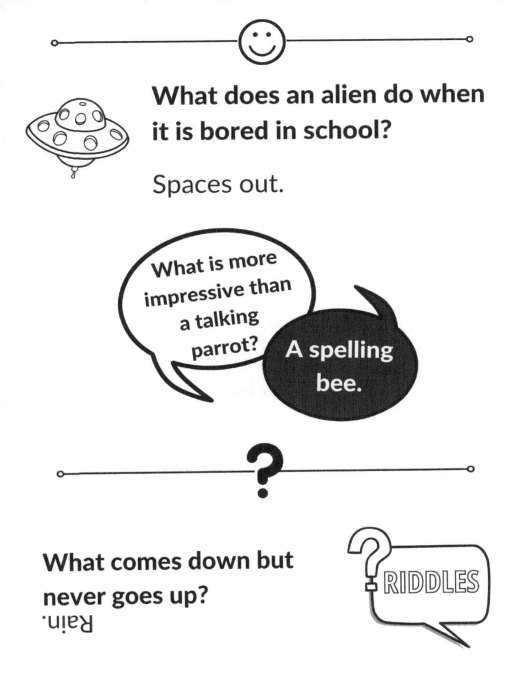

What does an alien do when it is bored in school?

Spaces out.

What is more impressive than a talking parrot?

A spelling bee.

What comes down but never goes up?
Rain.

RIDDLES

What has a bottom at the top of them?
Legs.

Who's there?
Sandy.
Sandy who?
Sandy Claus!

Who's there?
Tree.
Tree who?
Tree wise men.

Mommy made me eat my M&Ms.

Two monkeys were fighting over a banana. What happened?

Banana split!

What is orange and sounds like a parrot?

A carrot!

I never ask a question, but I am always answered. What am I?

A doorbell.

RIDDLES

People buy me to eat but then never eat me. What am I?

A plate.

Who's there?
Says.
Says who?
Says me!

Who's there?
Pears.
Pears who?
Pears the party!

I would if I could! But I
can't, so I won't!

Silly sheep weep and sleep.

Who's there?
Mary.
Mary who?
Mary Christmas!

Who's there?
A Fred.
A Fred who?
Are you a Fred of the
Big Bad Wolf?

Zebras zig and zebras zag.

**The crow flew over the river
with a lump of raw liver.**

Knock Knock!

Who's there?
Dishes
Dishes who?
Dishes your friend!

How did the bullet lose its job?

It got fired.

Smelly shoes and socks shock sisters.

TONGUE TWISTER

Fred fed Ted bread, and Ted fed Fred bread.

What is the best day to visit McDonald's?
Fry-Day!

What's a cow's favorite drink?

A s-moooo-thie.

This has bark that makes no sound.
A tree.

RIDDLES

What question can you never answer yes to?
Are you asleep yet?

Who's there?

Leaf

Leaf who?

Leaf me alone.

Who's there?

Cargo

Cargo who?

Cargo beep, beep!

**A snake sneaks to
seek a snack.**

**A big bug bit the little
beetle but the little beetle
bit the big bug back.**

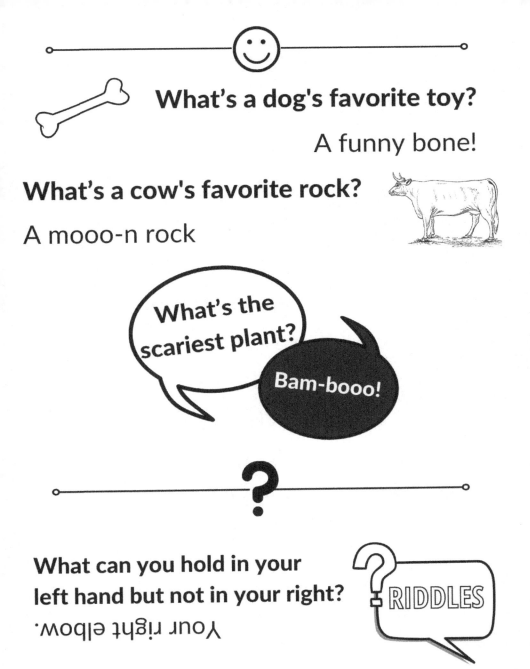

What's a dog's favorite toy?

A funny bone!

What's a cow's favorite rock?

A mooo-n rock

What's the scariest plant?

Bam-booo!

What can you hold in your left hand but not in your right?

Your right elbow.

RIDDLES

What is black when it's clean and white when it's dirty?

A chalkboard.

Who's there?
Who.
Who who?
I didn't know you
were an owl!

Who's there?
Flea.
Flea who?
Flea blind mice.

A sailor went to sea to see
what he could see.

What's a cow's favorite place to go?

The mooo-vies!

What's the scariest injury?

A booo-booo!

What do you call a dinosaur that is sleeping?

A dino-snore!

You see me once in June, twice in November, and not at all in May. What am I?

The letter "e".

RIDDLES

Which band never plays music?

A rubber band.

Who's there?
Monkey.
Monkey who?
Monkey see.
Monkey do.

Who's there?
Claws.
Claws who?
Claws the door,
I'm getting cold!

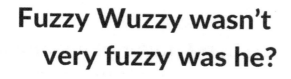

**Fuzzy Wuzzy wasn't
very fuzzy was he?**

What do birds give out on Halloween?

Tweets.

Why can't you ever tell a joke around glass?

It could crack up.

?

I have many teeth but will never bite. What am I?
A comb.

RIDDLES

I have a head and a tail but no body. What am I?
A coin.

Who's there?
Hello.
Hello who?
Hello Kitty!

Who's there?
Tank
Tank who?
You're welcome!

Toy boat. Toy boat. Toy boat.

If you want to buy, buy, if you
don't want to buy, bye-bye!

Why do we never tell jokes about pizza?

They're too cheesy.

What's a snake's strongest subject in school?

Hiss-tory.

What tastes better than it smells?
Your tongue.

RIDDLES

What fills a room without taking up any space?
Light.

Who's there?

Ty.

Ty who?

Ty up the dog
before he runs away.

Who's there?

Ants.

Ants who?

Ants in your pants!

**Fresh fried fish, fish fresh fried,
fried fish fresh, fish fried fresh.**

Where do cows go on Dec. 31st?

A moo year's eve party.

Where do you learn to make ice cream?

Sundae school.

What can you hold in your right hand but never in your left hand?

Your left hand.

Drop me and I'm sure to crack but lend me a smile and I'll certainly smile back. What am I?

A mirror.

Who's there?
Beezer.
Beezer who?
Beezer in your hair, ahhhh!!

Who's there?
Butter.
Butter who?
I butter not tell you!

Swan swam over the sea,
swim, swan, swim!
Swan swam back again.
Well swum, swan!

Why couldn't the duck pay for dinner?

Her bill was too big.

What animal dresses up and howls?

A wearwolf.

I have a neck with no head and two arms with no hands. What am I?

A shirt.

RIDDLES

DID YOU KNOW?

Lungs can float on water.

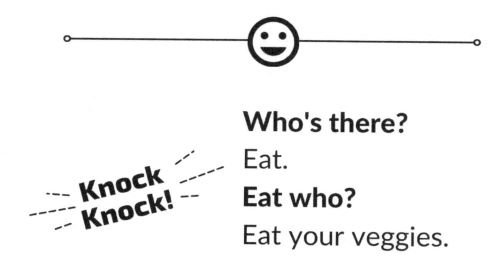

Who's there?
Eat.
Eat who?
Eat your veggies.

Who's there?
Lenny!
Lenny who?
Lenny in, I'm hungry!

Where she shines, she sits, and where she sits, she shines.

TONGUE TWISTER

How can a clam cram in a clean cream can?

What's blue and smells like red paint?

Blue paint.

What kind of music do balloons hate?

Pop.

**You can see it everyday,
But cannot touch it at will.
What is it?**
The sky.

RIDDLES

DID YOU KNOW?

**French fries originally come from
Belgium, not France.**

Selfish shellfish.

The top cop saw a cop top.

TONGUE TWISTER

**A big black bear sat
on a big black rug.**

**Knock
Knock!**

Who's there?
Nacho.
Nacho who?
Nacho cheese!

**Knock
Knock!**

Who's there?
Sid.
Sid who?
Sid down.
It's time to eat!

What do you call a pig that does karate?

A pork chop.

What do cats wear to bed?

Paw-jamas.

What did Mr. and Mrs. Hamburger name their daughter?

Patty

--- **DID YOU KNOW?** ---

Blue whales are the biggest animals on Earth.

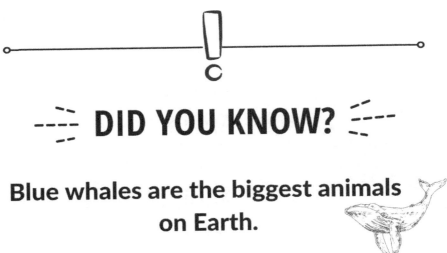

These sheep shouldn't
sleep in a shack;
Sheep should sleep in a shed.

The bottom of the butter
bucket is the buttered
bucket bottom.

Who's there?

Wool

Wool who?

Wool you get me
some water?

Who's there?

Annie.

Annie who?

Annie thing you can do,
I can do better!

What do you call a bear with no teeth?

A gummy bear.

What kind of bug is in the CIA?

A SPY-der.

What kind of money do mermaids use?

Sand dollars

DID YOU KNOW?

It has been tried and tested: it takes 364 licks to get to the center of a Tootsie Pop.

Can you can a can as
a canner can can a can?

The king would sing about a
ring that would go ding.

Knock Knock!

Who's there?
Winnie
Winnie who?
Winnie The Pooh!

Knock Knock!

Who's there?
Spell
Spell who?
W-H-O!

What mouse walks on two feet?

Mickey Mouse

What do you get when you put cheese next to some ducks?

Cheese and quackers.

☰ DID YOU KNOW? ☰

NFL Super Bowl referees get Super Bowl rings too.

How may saws could a see-saw saw if a see-saw could saw saws?

The great Greek grape growers grow great Greek grapes.

Who's there?
Tee
Tee who?
Tee hee!

Who's there?
Dime.
Dime who?
Dime to tell another knock-knock joke.

What do cats eat for breakfast?

Micekrispies.

Bake big batches of bitter brown bread.

TONGUE TWISTER

Crush grapes, grapes crush, crush grapes.

Knock Knock!

Who's there?
Berry
Berry who?
Berry nice too meet you.
Can I come in now?

Knock Knock!

Who's there?
Double
Double who?
W!

What's Superman's favorite drink?

PUNCH.

I was born on a short,
shiny, ship at shore.

If a dog chews shoes, whose
shoes does he choose?

**Knock
Knock!**

Who's there?
Rubber
Rubber who?
Rubber ducky!

**Knock
Knock!**

Who's there?
G.I.
G.I. who?
G.I. don't know?

What did one elevator yell to the other?

I'm falling!

How much dew does a dewdrop drop if dewdrops do drop dew?

TONGUE TWISTER

Knock Knock!

Who's there?
Abee

Abee who?
Abee C D E F G H I J
K L M N O P Q R S T
U V W X Y Z.

Knock Knock!

Who's there?
Icy

Icy who?
Icy you!

What always comes at the beginning of a parade?

The letter "P."

Busy buzzing bumble bees.

Nat the bat swat at Matt the gnat.

The soldier's shoulder surely hurts!

Who's there?

Wire

Wire who?

Wire you asking me?

Who's there?

Fang.

Fang who?

Fangs for letting me in!

What happened after the shark got famous?

He became a starfish.

What did the egg say to another egg?

"Have an eggselent day!"

While we were walking, we were watching window washers wash Washington's windows with warm washing water.

TONGUE TWISTER

Knock Knock!

Who's there?
Alli.
Alli who?
Alligator, that's who!

Knock Knock!

Who's there?
Hutch
Hutch who?
Bless you!

Leave Your Feedback on Amazon

Please think about leaving some feedback via a review on Amazon. It may only take a moment, but it really does mean the world for small businesses like mine.

Even if you did not enjoy this title, please let us know the reason(s) in your review so that we may improve this title and serve you better.

From the Publisher

Hayden Fox's mission is to create premium content for children that will help them expand their vocabulary, grow their imaginations, gain confidence, and share tons of laughs along the way.

Without you, however, this would not be possible, so we sincerely thank you for your purchase and for supporting our company mission.

Made in the USA
Middletown, DE
03 August 2022

70474129R00060